# CELEBRATION

D1197726

# CELEBRATION

*A salute to
a visiting artist*

———————

*edited by*

JIM FITZGERALD

VERITAS PUBLICATIONS

**50167**

First published 1979 by
Veritas Publications
Lower Abbey Street, Dublin 1

This Edition © 1979 Veritas Publications

Set in Baskerville type at the Dolmen Press
and printed in the Republic of Ireland by Cahill Printers Limited

Cover : St. Francis and the birds, sculpture by John Behan.
Photography by Wenzel Schürmann.

Designed by Liam Miller

ISBN 0 905092 72 4

# Contents

## AN EDITORIAL NOTICE

*Poets, by the very nature of the trade, are not at ease with authority. Each is at the epicentre of his own universe. Each is his own philosopher, seer, theologian, magician, authoritarian and pope.*

*Among my friends in the craft I have seen them celebrated, silenced, sometimes even cowed. But the best always have to hand,* in extremis, *the dreaded 'poet's curse'.*

*The late Patrick Kavanagh, on being refused a loan from a decent bank manager called Colthurst, said to me: 'That man is a first cousin of the man who shot Sheehy Skeffington.' 'Good God,' said I, 'is that true?' 'No it's not,' said Patrick, 'but I'm putting it about.'*

*This book could be 'A Mixed Blessing'.*

*Irish poets, north, south, east, and west; protestant, catholic, and dissenter, salute you, Karol Wojtyla: a poet who is also Pope.*

JIM FITZGERALD

# John Jordan

## LOLEK*

Czestochowa, Jasna Gora,
        Auschwitz, Nova Huta:
Archdiocesan Cracow:

Symphony of ashed flesh and steel and Mary,
Uncountable dark nights in the factory of death,
Salvos of laud on the Black Virgin's White Mountain
The people of God keen from metal with metamorphosed hearts.

Expectancy and rose of Christ's fair state
You have known it all:
Grease-paint, desk, sledge-hammer,
Arc-light, explosive, grammar,
Mickiewicz's mighty line,
More resounding than Wagnerian microphones,
Juliusz Slowacki in the Szkockas' drawing room,
Promethean Cyprian Norwid,
Poor Zegadlowicz who pained the clergy,
And Juan de la Cruz wrestling,
Parched in a tawny landscape,
With the Angel of Faith.

You expect much faith from Patrick's children
In this our pleasant land of Country and Western singers,
So great a hope as yours must find it.
And meantime—while the phones ring and the keys tap and the
        words spawn—
Let the chisellers† and the unstained
Sing a carol for Karol:
'May Holy Ireland be holier,
Perhaps even made whole.'

*The Feast of the Assumption, 1979*

*Pope John Paul II's boyhood name.
†Dublin expression for street urchins.

Seamus Heaney

SWEENEY PRAISES THE TREES

The branchy leafy oak-tree
is highest in the wood,
the shooting hazel bushes
hide sweet hazel-nuts.

The alder is my darling,
all thornless in the gap,
some milk of human kindness
coursing in its sap.

The blackthorn is a jaggy creel,
stippled with dark sloes;
green watercress is thatch on wells
where the drinking blackbird goes.

Sweetest of the leafy stalks,
the vetches strew the pathway;
the oyster-grass is my delight
and the wild strawberry.

Low-set clumps of apple-trees
drum down fruit when shaken;
scarlet berries clot like blood
on mountain rowan.

Briars curl in sideways,
arch a stickle back,
draw blood, and curl back innocent
to sneak the next attack.

The yew-tree in each churchyard
wraps night in its dark hood.
ivy is a shadowy
genius of the wood.

Holly rears its windbreak,
a door in winter's face;
life-blood on a spear-shaft
darkens the grain of ash.

Birch-tree, smooth and pale-skinned,
delicious to the breeze,
high twigs plait and crown it
the queen of trees.

The aspen pales
and whispers, hesitates:
a thousand frightened scuts
race in its leaves.

But what disturbs me most
in the living wood
is the swishing to and fro
of an oak-rod.

*from the Middle Irish*

[11]

Pearse Hutchinson

## HOMAGE TO JOSE MARTI

The Spanish bishop covets
pillars for his altar:
in my church, on the hill,
elm is altar.

Floor is fern,
walls birch,
the light comes down
from the blue ceiling.

At night the bishop
goes out to sing;
he rides, in silence,
on a pine-kernel.

I sleep sound
on a stone bed;
a bee grazes my lips,
and in my body the world grows.

Tell the blind bishop,
the old bishop of Spain,
to come to my church
on the hill.

Eiléan Ní Chuilleanáin

## THE APPARITION

The circular white sun
Leapt overhead and grew
Red as a rose, darkening slowly blue.
And the crowd wept, shivering,
Standing there in the cold.

The sharp-eyed girl miraculously
Cured by a beggar passed the word along.
Water, she said, and they found a spring
Where all before was dry.
They filled the jars with the water.

All will be forgiven, good and evil together.
You are all my Children. Come back
In mist or snow, here it will be warm.
And forget the perishing cold,
The savage light of day.

Every Friday at noon the same;
The trains were full of people in the evenings
Going north with gallons of sour water.

Tomás Mac Síomóin

## MURA . . .

Mura gcuirir claidheamh an chlampair id' thruaill,
Mura scoirir ded' strí in aghaidh na taoille,
Mura ngéillir do fháisceadh fuar Nióbe
Cén chaoi a' dtomhaisfir rún
A croí-siúd,
Nó a h-uimhir 'tá scríofa
Ar ghaoth is ar thaoille,
Nó a port ná staonann
Ar bhéal an tsalainn?

Mura gcuirir claidheamh an chlampair id' thruaill,
Gliúcaí a bheas ionat go broinn na brácha,
Ag seasamh mar leathcheann ar theallach Eleusis,
Id' straeire strusach gan teacht i láthair,
Is tú foclach, fairgseach
I bhfara an díamhaire.


Lúnasa 1979

UNLESS . . .

Unless you sheathe that rowdy sword
And cease your fight against the tide
And surrender to Niobe's cold embrace
How can you know the secret
Of Niobe's heart,
Her number written
On wind and tide
Or the song unceasing
On her mouth of salt?

Unless you sheathe that rowdy sword
The voyeur's fate shall be yours forever —
Buffoon standing on the threshold of Eleusis —
A wanderer, demented,
Squinting, wordy
In the presence of the mystery!

August 1979

John Montague

CATHEDRAL TOWN

I lived in Armagh
In a time of war    the most dreamy
Time of my life    Beyond your walls
   Shape of lost surety
   My future lay

Looming cathedral
Memory shapes you in the air
On a night when a cutting wind
   Marks the glass
   With bursts of rain

Tall guardian
Of my childhood in the Ulster
Night    overhanging Patrick's city
   Its huddled roofs
   Fringed with rain

As the iron bell
Swings out again    each quarter's
Notes dwindling down a shaft
   Of present and past
   To drowning monotone

*after a poem by François Monod*, 'Reims'

[16]

Eiléan Ní Chuilleanáin

LUCINA SCHYNNING IN SILENCE OF THE NIGHT . . .

Moon shining in silence of the night
The heaven being all full of stars
I was reading my book in a ruin
By a sour candle, without roast meat or music
Strong drink or a shield from the air
Blowing in the crazed window, and I felt
Moonlight on my head, clear after three days' rain.

I washed in cold water; it was orange, channelled down bogs
Dipped between cresses.
The bats flew through my room where I slept safely.
Sheep stared at me when I woke.

Behind me the waves of darkness lay, the plague
Of mice, plague of beetles
Crawling out of the spines of books,
Plague shadowing pale faces with clay
The disease of the moon gone astray.

In the desert I relaxed, amazed
As the mosaic beasts on the chapel floor
When Cromwell had departed, and they saw
The sky growing through the hole in the roof.

Sheepdogs embraced me; the grasshopper
Returned with lark and bee.
I looked down between hedges of high thorn and saw
The hare, absorbed, sitting still
In the middle of the track; I heard
Again the chirp of the stream running.

# John Montague

## A FOOTNOTE ON MONASTICISM:
### DINGLE PENINSULA

In certain places, still, surprisingly, you come
Upon them, resting like old straw hats set down
Beside the sea, weather-beaten but enduring
For a dozen centuries: here the mound
That was the roof has slithered in
And the outlines you can barely trace:
Nor does it matter since every wilderness
Along this rocky coast retains more signs
In ragged groupings of these cells and caves,
Of where the hermits, fiercely dispossessed,
Found refuge among gulls and rocks
The incessant prayer of nearby waves.

Among darkening rocks he prayed,
Body chastened and absurd,
An earth-bound dragging space
His spirit blundered like a bird:
Hands, specialised by prayer,
Like uplifted chalices,
Nightly proferring the self
To soundless, perfect messengers.

There are times, certainly, looking through a window
At amiable clustered humanity, or scanning
The leaves of some old book, that one might wish
To join their number, start a new and fashionable
Sect beside the Celtic sea, long favourable
To dreams and dreamers; anchorites whose love

Was selfishly alone, a matter so great
That only to stone could they whisper it:
Breaking the obstinate structure of flesh
With routine of vigil and fast,
Till water-cress stirred on the palate
Like the movement of a ghost.

In ceaseless labour of the spirit,
Isolate, unblessed;
Until quietude of the senses
Announces presence of a guest;
Desolation final,
Rock within and rock without
Till from the stubborn rock of the heart
The purifying waters spurt.

1953

Paul Muldoon

## OUR LADY OF ARDBOE

### I

Just there, in a corner of the whin-field,
Just where the thistles bloom.
She stood there as in Bethlehem
One night in nineteen fifty-three or four.

The girl leaning over the half-door
Saw the cattle kneel, and herself knelt.

### II

I suppose that a farmer's youngest daughter
Might, as well as the next, unravel
The winding road to Christ's navel.

Who's to know what's knowable?
Milk from the Virgin Mother's breast,
A feather off the Holy Ghost?
The fairy thorn? The holy well?

Our simple wish for there being more to life
Than a job, a car, a house, a wife —
The fixity of running water.

For I like to think, as I step these acres,
That a holy well is no more shallow
Nor plummetless than the pools of Shiloh,
The fairy thorn no less true than the Cross.

## III

Mother of our Creator, Mother of our Saviour,
Mother most amiable, Mother most admirable.
Virgin most prudent, Virgin most venerable,
Mother inviolate, Mother undefiled.

And I walk waist-deep among purples and golds
With one arm as long as the other.

Eavan Boland

*for Eavan Frances*

This is dawn.
Believe me
This is your season, little daughter:
The moment daisies open,
The hour mercurial rainwater
Makes a mirror for sparrows.
It's time to drown our sorrows.

I tiptoe in.
I lift you up
Wriggling
In your rosy, zipped sleeper.
Yes this is the hour
For the early bird and me
When finder is keeper.

I crook the bottle.
How you suckle!
This is the best I can be:
Housewife
To this nursery
Where you hold on,
Dear life.

A silt of milk.
The last suck.
And now your eyes are open,
Birth-coloured and offended.

Earth wakes,
You go back to sleep.
The feed is ended:

Worms turn.
Stars go in.
Even the moon is losing face.
Poplars stilt for dawn
And we begin
The long fall from grace.
I tuck you in.

# Brendan Kennelly

## THE WORK WAS COMING OUT RIGHT

Anne Mulvihill lifted the box
Containing the shroud
Down from the top of the wardrobe,
Laid the shroud out on the table,
Ironed it with love
Or a care that looked like love.
She'd ironed clothes for husband and children
All the long years
And would again
But this was different work.
She pressed every inch of the brown shroud
As though her life depended on it.
Not once did she lift her eyes
But pressed the cloth with her mind
As if she would get her death in order
Or consecrate her ignorance
Of past and future dying.
She pressed
                    with her heart's patience in her face,
Her working days,
Love-making nights,
Beasts' and children's cries,
The seasons' rhythms in her fingers,
Fields changing colours
Like tired beliefs
Impassioned from within.
She pressed with her knowledge of sin,
Her taste of grace,
Her bargaining power with heaven,
Her struggle with one who struggled with earth.

She hummed a tune as she pressed
Knowing the work was coming out right.
Then she lifted the shroud
Like a chalice of work
Up to the light
Admiring the shape in silence.

It was done,

Perfect as her smile
When she stood the hot iron on its end
To cool.

Pearse Hutchinson

An bhfaca tú Íosa
ag ithe fíona
le teann an uabhair
i dteannta Iúdais?

An bhfaca tú Muire
ag ól ime
le neart náire
i dteannta Mháire?

Ní iarrfad maitheamh
go h-umhal ar shagart
i mbosca dorcha
tromdonn docht a
rinne fá ghrásta
fear éigin cráite.

Ní gheobhad faoiseamh
ach oiread uaibhse,
a lucht síormhaoite
na leapan folaimhe;
ná ní chuirfead i bhfolach mo
náire ghonta
fád chlúmhsa, a dhuine
nár chaill riamh suirí.

Ar mo chomharsain, ar mo dhéithe,
ar chumhacht na gréine,
ar na daoine a ghoineas-sa,
ar na pianta a cuireadh orm,
ar an bhfear sa sagart,
ar mo scáthán briste,
iarrfad maitheamh.

# John Hewitt

## WHIT MONDAY

The small girls hurried to the hill-top church,
their confirmation dresses fluttering
in the late sun. Before the shadowed porch
neat-fingered mothers knotted lace and string
and pinned each floral coronet in place;
while the dark-suited fathers stood apart
pride and affection on each polished face :
it seemed as though some play were poised to start,
when the last swift had scoured the humming air.

Yet this was Poland, and the time was now;
and I, who pray too seldom, felt a prayer
take all my will, that providence allow,
or dialectic, or whatever name
men put upon time's enginery, permit
this scene to re-enact itself, the same,
so long as any heart finds grace in it.

Roy McFadden

### SAINT FRANCIS AND THE BIRDS

Hearing him, the birds came in a crowd,
Wing upon wing, from stone and blade and twig,
From tilted leaf and thorn and lumbering cloud,
Falling from hill, soaring from meadowland,
Wing upon widening wing, until the air
Wrinkled with sound and ran like watery sand
Round the sky's gleaming bowl. Then, like a flower
They swung, hill-blue and tremulous, each wing
A petal palpitating in a shower
Of words, till he beneath felt the stale crust
Of self crinkle and crumble and his words
Assume an independence, pure and cold,
Cageless, immaculate, one with the birds
Fattening their throats in song. Identity
Lost, he stood in swollen ecstasy.

Richard Murphy

A shoulder of rock
Sticks high up out of the sea,
A fisherman's mark
For lobster and blue-shark.

Fissile and stark
The crust is flaking off,
Seal-rock, gull-rock,
Cove and cliff.

Dark mounds of mica schist,
A lake, mill and chapel,
Roofless, one gable smashed,
Lie ringed with rubble.

An older calm,
The kiss of rock and grass,
Pink thrift and white sea-campion,
Flowers in the dead place.

Day keeps lit a flare
Round the north pole all night
Like brushing long wavy hair
Petrels quiver in flight.

Quietly as the rustle
Of an arm entering a sleeve,
They slip down to nest
Under altar-stone or grave.

Round the wrecked laura
Needles flicker
Tacking air, quicker and quicker
To rock, sea and star.

Tomás Mac Síomóin

## AN TOST

Nuair a dhéanair dem' chnámha
Fráma cruite,
Nuair a dhéanair dem' cheann
An bosca ceoil,
Nuair a dhéanair dem' mhéara
Fearas stoite,
Nuair a dhéanair dem' néaróg
A h-aonsreang óir,

Nuair a theannair isteach
Is nuair fháiscir go dlúth mé,
Nuair a chasair do cheol
Tri bhéal an fhile,
A Thiarna na bhFlaitheas,
Ní mór é an t-íonadh
Do bhuanphort a bhraith
Faoi sheal a shiolla!

Meitheamh 1979

When You build Your harpframe
From these — my bones,
And make of this skull
Its sounding box,
Make of these neurons
Its golden strings,
Make of my nails
A plectrum,

And, gripping me tightly,
Through a poet's mouth sing
Your song,
O Jesu mild, our Saviour,
What wonder then
Your eternal song
Beneath a fleeting syllable?

June 1979

Richard Murphy

GRANITE GLOBE

Straining my back
Seven times I've lifted you
Up to my thighs

There are men
Who've put you sitting
High on their shoulders

It looks as if you'd been
Lopped
Off the top of a column

Then used as a quern
Kicked around
Buried

An archaeologist
Taped you
And wrote you down

He said
You're an oblate spheroid
Does it matter?

Whoever carved you
Gave you all
The time in the world

Michael Longley

## THE LINEN WORKERS

Christ's teeth ascended with him into heaven :
Through a cavity in one of his molars
The wind whistles : he is fastened for ever
By his exposed canines to a wintry sky.

I am blinded by the blaze of that smile
And by the memory of my father's false teeth
Brimming in their tumbler : they wore bubbles
And, outside of his body, a deadly grin.

When they massacred the ten linen workers
There fell on the road beside them spectacles,
Wallets, small change, and a set of dentures :
Blood, food particles, the bread, the wine.

Before I can bury my father once again
I must polish the spectacles, balance them
Upon his nose, fill his pockets with money
And into his dead mouth slip the set of teeth.

# Fear Dorcha Ó Mealláin, c. 1650

## "TO HELL OR TO CONNACHT"

Following an Act of the English Parliament passed in 1652 —
'All Catholics (and many Protestant Royalists) above the rank of
tradesman or labourer were to remove themselves and their families
into Connacht and Clare, where they were given small allotments.
Any of those ordered away found east of the Shannon after May 1st
1654, might be killed by whoever met them. The move had to be
made mostly in Winter. The season was very severe, and the roads
almost impassable. Hundreds perished on the way.' (*Duanaire
Gaeilge II*, p. 134, R. Ní Ógáin.)

The poem is a prayer for the journey, with special reference to
these events.

### AN DIBIRT GO CONNACHTA

In ainm an Athar go mbuaidh,
   in ainm an Mhic fuair an phian,
in ainm an Spioraid Naoimh le neart,
   Muire 's a Mac linn ag triall.

Mícheál feartach ár gcuid stóir,
   Muire Ógh 's an dá aspal déag,
Brighid, Pádraig agus Eoin —
   is maith an lón creideamh Dé.

Colam Cille feartach caomh,
   's Colmán mhac Aoidh, ceann na gcliar,
beid linn uile ar aon tslí
   's ná bígí ag caoi fá dhul siar.

Nach dtuigeann sibh, a bhráithre gaoil
   cúrsaí an tsaoil le fada buan? —
gé mór atá 'nár seilbh,
   beag bheas linn ag dul san uaigh.

Thomas Kinsella
*from the Irish of F. Ó Mealláin*

EXODUS TO CONNACHT

In the name of the Father full of virtue,
   in the name of the Son Who suffered pain,
in the name of the Holy Ghost in power,
   Mary and her Son be with us.

Our sole possessions: Michael of miracles,
   the Virgin Mary, the twelve apostles,
Brigid, Patrick and Saint John
   — and fine rations: faith in God.

Sweet Colm Cille of miracles too,
   and Colmán Mac Aoidh, poets' patron,
will all be with us on our way.
   Do not bewail our journey West.

Brothers mine, do you not see
   the ways of the world a while now?
However much we may possess
   we'll go with little into the grave.

Uirscéal as sin tuigthear libh:
   clann Israel a bhean le Dia,
san Éigipt cé bhí i mbroid,
   furtacht go grod a fuair siad.

Do-chuadar tríd an mhuir mhóir,
   go ndearnadh dhóibh ród nár ghann,
gur éirigh an fhairrge ghlas
   mar charraig 'mach os a gceann.

Iar ndul dhóibhsin fó thír
   fuair siad cóir ó Rí na rann,
furtacht, cabhair agus biadh
   ón Dia bhí riamh is tá ann.

Fuaradar ó neamh mar lón
   cruithneachta mhór — stór nár bheag —
mil dá chur mar cheo,
   uisce go leor ag teacht as creig.

Amhlaidh sin do-ghéanfar libh:
   do-ghéabhaidh sibh gach maith ar dtús;
atá bhur ndúithche ar neamh,
   's ná bígí leamh in bhur gcúis.

A chlann chroí, déanaidh seasamh,
   's ná bígí ag ceasnamh le hanró;
Maoise a fuair ar agaill —
   cead a chreidimh ó Pharó.

Ionann Dia dhúinn agus dhóibh,
   aon Dia fós do bhí 'gus tá;
ionann Dia abhus agus thiar,
   aon Dia riamh is bheas go bráth.

Consider a parable of this:
    Israel's people, God's own,
although they were in bonds in Egypt,
    found in time a prompt release.

Through the mighty sea they passed,
    an ample road was made for them,
then the grey-green ocean rose
    out there above them like a rock.

When they came to dry land
    the King of Heaven minded them
— relief, succour and nourishment
    from the God who ever was and is.

Food from Heaven they received:
    great wheat, in no small measure,
honey settling like a mist,
    abundant water out of rock.

Likewise it shall be done to you:
    all good things shall first be yours.
Heaven is your inheritance.
    Be not faint-hearted in your faith.

People of my heart, stand steady,
    don't complain of your distress.
Moses got what he requested,
    religious freedom — and from Pharaoh.

Identical their God and ours.
    One God there was and still remains.
Here or Westward God is one,
    one God ever and shall be.

Má ghoirthear dhaoibhse Páipis,
   cuiridh fáilte re bhur ngairm;
tugaidh foighead don Ardrí —
   *Deo gratias*, maith an t-ainm.

A Dhia atá fial, a thriath na mbeannachta,
féach na Gaeil go léir gan bharanta;
má táimid ag triall siar go Connachta,
fágmaid 'nár ndiaidh fó chian ár seanchairde.

If they call you 'Papishes'
  accept it gladly for a title.
Patience, for the High King's sake.
  *Deo Gratias*, good the name!

God Who art generous, O Prince of Blessings,
behold the Gael, stripped of authority.
Now as we journey Westward into Connacht
old friends we'll leave behind us in their grief.

Robert O'Donoghue

## UNION

Most democratic worm
partial to orange as
to green and the clay

your common porridge
now — you paidup members
of the common club

you bombplanting bastards
and you the blasted are all
one now and how does it feel

to lie with your victim
in one small bed his blood
your blood and the two

burst brains leaping
together sharing the
selfsame rat

lying together like lovers
at last what does it feel
to be one.

Sydney Bernard Smith

## POLITICAL MEETING

a Heidelberg cellar, leftover
from the middle ages, the young
in their monastic handmedowns
black or drab or bedraggled like
the society for which they are in mourning,
soulful glances of reproach and self-reproach,
scorn and self-scorn.
we watch
three scrappy reels of film on Northern Ireland
with out-of-phase German dubbing heaped onto
the backyards of Derry and Belfast.

they with their quadrantamarx-pocket-reckoners
and dialectoscopes frown away
irrelevant untidy and dammit unnecessary
facts. they refine a crystal present.
they plot the angle and define the cant
of a future revolutionary hypoteneuse.

their own future alarms them they need to be right
unrest stirs in the unknown country of
their own meat, chemicals that prick new cells
into being, like a bloodstain.
their eyes are alert for dangers out front
while in behind them the war bumbles
merrily away. they hold up to the light
in a phial distilled and clarified reason
almost invisible in solution.

after the street-rubble on the screen
after the black the white the gray
running jumping and lying very still.
like one dark body with a smashed head
resting in the lightened roadway,
beside it lay a shadow knocked out of shape
the black black blood pooled in an
all-too-real parody of man.

# Michael Davitt

### TARRAING AN CUIRTIN A MHAMA

cé phleanáil an fáiltiú seo a Mhama
cé smaoinigh ar scigdhráma
cén fáth amharclann
aghaidheanna fidil, cnaguirlisí, spotsholas
cé tá ag scréachaíl
cé leis an lámh mhór
a stracann as do bhroinn ghrámhar
isteach in ifreann mé
cá bhfuil do chíoch
tarraing an cuirtín a Mhama
impím ort

Paul Durcan

*to Karol Wojtyla*

When I was thirteen I broke my leg.

Being the sensible, superstitious old lady that she was,
My Aunt Sarah knew that, while to know God was good,
To get the Ear of His Mother was a more practical step:
Kneeling on the flagstone floor of her kitchen, all teaspoons and
    whins,
Outspoken as Moses, she called out Litanies to Our Lady:
The trick was to circumambulate the Shrine fifteen times
Repeating the rosary, telling your beads:
And so: that is how I came to be
Hopping round Knock Shrine in the Falling Rain.

In the Heel of that Spiritual Hunt
I became a Falling Figure clinging to the Shrine Wall
While Mayo rain pelleted down jamming and jetting:
And, while all the stalls — of relics, and phials of holy water,
And souvenir grottos, and souvenir postcards,
And spheres which, when shaken, shook with fairy snow,
And sticks of Knock Rock —
Were being folded-up for the day, I veered on
Falling round Knock Shrine in the Hopping Rain.

*Gable, O Gable, is there no Respite to thy Mercy?*

The trick did not work
But that is scarcely the point:
That day was a crucial day
In my hedge school of belief

In the Potential of Miracle,
In the Actuality of Vision :
And, therefore, I am grateful
For my plateful
Of Hopping round Knock Shrine in the Falling Rain.

# Contributors

**Eavan Boland**  Published her first collection of poems — *New Territory* at 22. In 1968 was awarded the Macaulay fellowship for poetry. Published a further collection of poems, *The War Horse* (Gollancz) 1975. Is at present preparing her new book, *In Her Own Image*, for publication in the Spring. Is married with two children.

**Michael Davitt** (1950–    )  Rugadh i gCorcaigh. Céim sa léann Ceilteach i gColáiste Ollscoile Chorcaí 1971. Eagarthóir na hirise filíochta *Innti*. Bainisteoir ar an ógfhéile Slógadh 1974–1978.
Ag gabháil d'obair na n-ealaíon faoi láthair i nGael linn.

**Paul Durcan** (1944–    )  Born Dublin. Educated at University College Cork. Published first 1967, *Endsville*, a collection shared with Brian Lynch. 1974 won the Patrick Kavanagh Award for Poetry. Published his first solo collection of poems, *O Westport in the Light of Asia Minor*, 1975. 1976 was awarded an Arts Council Bursary for Creative Writing. Since then has had two further collections published : *Teresa's Bar* (Gallery Press), and *Sam's Cross* (Profile). Married, with two children, and lives in Cork.

**Seamus Heaney** (1939–    )  A Northerner, now lives in Dublin and is head of the English Department at Carysfort College. Published works include
> *Death of a Naturalist* (Faber and Faber) 1968
> *Door into the Dark* (Faber and Faber) 1969
> *Wintering Out* (Faber and Faber) 1972
> *North* (Faber and Faber) 1975
> *After Summer* (Deerfield Press and Gallery Press) 1978

**John Hewitt** (1907–    )  Born in Belfast. Educated at Queen's University, Belfast. Collected poems were published 1968. Most recent book of poems, *The Rain Dance*, was published in 1978 by Blackstaff Press. Has been writer-in-residence at Queen's University since 1976.

**Pearse Hutchinson** (1927–     ) Writes in Irish and in English. After three years in England came home to Dublin in 1974. Publications include

>   *Tongue without Hands* (Dolmen) 1963
>   *Expansions* (Dolmen) 1969
>   *Faoistin Bhacach* (Clóchomhar) 1969
>   *Watching the Morning Grow* (Gallery Press)
>   *Josep Carner: 30 poems — From Catalan* (Dolphin Books Oxford)
>   *Friend Songs: Medieval Love Poems from Galaicoportuguese* (New Writers' Press)

**John Jordan** (1930–     ) Born in Dublin. Poet, university lecturer, critic, broadcaster. Publications include

>   *Patrician Stations* (New Writers' Press) 1971
>   *Blood Stations* (New Writers' Press) 1976
>   *A Raft from Flotsam '78* (Gallery Press) 1978

**Brendan Kennelly** (1936–     ) Born in Ballylongford, Co. Kerry. Educated at Trinity College, Dublin, and at Leeds University. Publications include

>   *Collection One* (1966)
>   *Selected Poems* (1969)
>   *Love Cry* (1972)
>   *Shelley in Dublin* (1974)
>   *Islandman* (1976)
>   *A Small Light* (1979)

Is Professor of Modern Literature at Trinity College.

**Thomas Kinsella** (1929–     )
Publications include

>   *Another September* (1958)
>   *Downstream* (1962)
>   *Wormwood* (1966)
>   *Nightwalker and other Poems* (1968)

**Michael Longley** (1939–     ) Lives in Belfast. Works for Arts Council Northern Ireland. Educated Belfast and Trinity College Dublin. Co-winner with Derek Mahon of Gregory Award 1965.

Published works include
> *No Continuing City* (Macmillan) 1969
> *An Exploded View* (Gollancz) 1973
> *Man Lying on a Wall* (Gollancz) 1976

Latest book of poems, *The Echo Gate*, to be published in 1979.

**Roy McFadden** (1922–    ) Lives in Belfast. A lawyer by profession. Published works include
> *Swords and Ploughshares* (1943)
> *Flowers for a Lady* (1945)
> *Elegy for the Dead of the Princess Victoria* (1953)
> *The Garryowen* (1977)
> *Verifications* (1977)
> *A Watching Brief* (1979)

**Tomás Mac Síomóin**   Rugadh i mBleá Cliath. Oideachas in Éirinn, san Ísiltir agus in America. Léachtóir le Bitheolaíocht. Leabhar foilsithe, *Damhna* (Sairséal agus Dill) Duais Chomhairle Ealaíona 1970. Dhá leabhar ag na foilsitheoirí faoi láthair.

**John Montague** (1929–    ) Born in New York. Educated in University College Dublin where he has been a visiting lecturer. Published collections include
> *Poisoned Lands* (Dolmen) 1961
> *A Chosen Light* (Dolmen) 1967
> *Tides* (Dolmen)
> *The Rough Field* (Dolmen) 1972
> *A Slow Dance* (Dolmen)
> *The Leap* (Deerfield and Gallery Press) 1979

Now lives in Cork and teaches at University College Cork.

**Paul Muldoon**   Born County Armagh 1951. Educated Queen's University Belfast. Won the Gregory Award for Poetry 1972. Published collections include
> *New Weather* (Faber and Faber) 1973
> *Mules* (Faber and Faber) 1977

Works as a radio producer, B.B.C. Belfast.

[51]

**Richard Murphy** (1927–    ) Born Co. Galway. Æ Memorial Award 1951. Publications include
> *Sailing to an Island* (Faber and Faber) 1963
> *The Battle of Aughrim* (Faber and Faber) 1968
> *High Island* (Faber and Harper and Rowe) 1974
> *Selected Poems* (Faber and Faber) 1979

Has lived most of his life in Connemara.

**Eiléan Ní Chuilleanáin** (1942–    ) Born Cork city. Educated at University College Cork and at Oxford. Received Irish Times Award for Poetry 1966. Received Patrick Kavanagh Award for first collection, *Acts and Monuments* (Gallery Press). Publications include
> *Site of Ambush* (Gallery Press) 1975
> *The Second Voyage* (Gallery Press) 1977
> *Cork*, with drawings by Brian Lalor, 1977

Now a lecturer in Trinity College Dublin.

**Robert O'Donoghue** (1929–    ) Poet, playwright and journalist. A Corkman. Married with five sons.

**Sydney Bernard Smith** (1936–    ) Grew up in Portstewart. Has lived since 1971 in Inisbofin, Co. Galway. Publications include
> *Girl with Violin*, poems
> *Sherca*, play
> *The Fabulous Life of Guillaume Apollinaire*
>   (collaborate translation)
> *Priorities*, poems (Raven Arts) 1979
> *The Book of Shannow* (forthcoming Dolmen)

\*

**Jim FitzGerald** (1929–    ) Has been a theatre and television director for thirty years in Ireland, England, France, Holland, etc. Has been a noted controversialist, but at the moment is very happy to join in this celebratory enterprise.

# Acknowledgements

For permission to reprint the poems in this anthology, acknowledgement is made to the following :

Eavan Boland : 'Night Feed' — to the author; Michael Davitt : 'Tarraing an Cuirtín a Mhama' — to the author; Paul Durcan : 'Hopping Round Knock Shrine in the Falling Rain' 1958 — to the author; Seamus Heaney : 'Sweeney Praises the Trees' — to the author; John Hewitt : 'Whit Monday' from *Collected Poems* — to the author; Pearse Hutchinson : 'Fiafraí' and 'Maitheamh', both from *Faoistin Bhacach* — to An Clóchomhar; 'Homage to José Marti' from *Watching the Morning Grow* — to Gallery Press; John Jordan : 'Lolek' — to the author; Brendan Kennelly : 'The Work was Coming Out Right'—to the author; Thomas Kinsella : 'Exodus to Connacht' — to the author; Michael Longley : 'The Linen Workers' — to the author; Roy McFadden : 'Saint Francis and the Birds' — to the author; Tomás Mac Síomóin : 'An Tost' and translation—to the author; 'Mura' and translation—to the author; John Montague : 'Cathedral Town' and 'A Footnote on Monasticism—Dingle Peninsula'—from *Poisoned Lands*—to The Dolmen Press; Paul Muldoon : 'Our Lady of Ardboe' from *Mules* — to Faber and Faber Ltd.; Richard Murphy : 'High Island' and 'Granite Globe' from *Selected Poems* — to Faber and Faber Ltd.; Eiléan Ní Chuilleanáin : 'The Apparition' from *Site of Ambush* — to Gallery Press; 'Lucina Schynning in Silence of the Night' from *Site of Ambush* — to Gallery Press; Robert O'Donoghue : 'Union' — to *Cyphers/Threshold*; Sydney Bernard Smith : 'Political Meeting' from *Priorities* — to Raven Arts.